EGYPT'S Ancient Secrets

KING TUT
The Hidden Tomb

by Ruth Owen

Consultant: Dr. Christopher Naunton
Egyptologist

BEARPORT
PUBLISHING

New York, New York

Credits

Cover and Title Page, © Jose Lucas/Alamy; 4, © David Cole/Alamy; 5, © Reuters/Alamy and © Chudodecor/Shutterstock; 6R, © Ariadne Van Zandbergen/Alamy; 7L, © Vladimir Wrangel/Shutterstock; 7R, © Danita Delimont/Alamy; 8–9, © Dorling Kindersley/Getty Images; 9B, © Francesco de Marco/Shutterstock; 10, © Sandro Vannini/Getty Images; 11T, © Heritage Image Partnership Ltd/Alamy; 11B, © De Agostini/W. Buss/Getty Images; 12, © The Keasbury-Gordon Photograph Archive/Alamy; 13, © The Keasbury-Gordon Photograph Archive/Alamy; 14T, © Robert Harding/Alamy; 14B, © Leemage/Getty Images; 15, © Griffith Institute, University of Oxford; 16L, © The Print Collector/Alamy; 16R, © Jose Lucas/Alamy; 17L, © Griffith Institute, University of Oxford, colorized by Dynamichrome; 17R, © Leemage/Getty Images; 18, © Griffith Institute, University of Oxford, colorized by Dynamichrome; 19T, © Griffith Institute, University of Oxford, colorized by Dynamichrome; 19B, © Jose Lucas/Alamy; 20, © Robert Harding/Getty Images; 21L, © Kenneth Garrett/National Geographic Creative; 21R, © epa european pressphoto agency b.v./Alamy; 22L, © Werner Forman/Getty Images; 22R, © Robert Harding/Getty Images; 23L, © Alessandro Vannini/Getty Images; 23R, © Robert Harding/Alamy; 24, © Danita Delimont/Alamy; 25, © De Agostini/A. Jemolo/Getty Images; 26, © Egyptian/Getty Images; 27, © Naeblys/Alamy; 28T, © Jose Lucas/Alamy; 28B, © epa european pressphoto agency b.v./Alamy; 29T, © tkachuk/Shutterstock; 29B, © epa european pressphoto agency b.v./Alamy; 31, © Robert Harding/Getty Images.

Publisher: Kenn Goin
Senior Editor: Joyce Tavolacci
Creative Director: Spencer Brinker
Photo Researcher: Ruby Tuesday Books Ltd

Library of Congress Cataloging-in-Publication Data

Names: Owen, Ruth, 1967– author.
Title: King Tut : the hidden tomb / by Ruth Owen.
Other titles: Egypt's ancient secrets.
Description: New York, New York : Bearport Publishing Company, 2017. |
    Series: Egypt's ancient secrets | Includes bibliographical references and
    index.
Identifiers: LCCN 2016049177 (print) | LCCN 2016051601 (ebook) | ISBN
    9781684020225 (library) | ISBN 9781684020744 (ebook)
Subjects: LCSH: Tutankhamen, King of Egypt—Juvenile literature. |
    Tutankhamen, King of Egypt—Tomb—Juvenile literature. | Excavations
    (Archaeology)—Egypt—Valley of the Kings—Juvenile literature.
Classification: LCC DT87.5 .O94 2017 (print) | LCC DT87.5 (ebook) | DDC
    932/.014092 [B] —dc23
LC record available at https://lccn.loc.gov/2016049177

For more information, write to Bearport Publishing Company, Inc.,
45 West 21st Street, Suite 3B, New York, New York 10010.
Printed in the United States of America.

10 9 8 7 6 5 4 3 2 1

Contents

Gold Everywhere!

It was late afternoon on November 26, 1922, in the Egyptian desert. In an underground passageway below the Valley of the Kings, British **archaeologist** Howard Carter worked in **tense** silence. As sweat trickled down his face, he used a tool to chip a hole in a stone doorway.

For five years, Carter had been searching for the hidden **tomb** of the ancient Egyptian **pharaoh**, Tutankhamen (*too*-tahn-KAH-men). Finally, Carter had discovered a doorway that might lead to the tomb. Carefully, he lifted a candle to the hole and peered into the darkness.

The Valley of the Kings is a large cemetery, or burial place, in the Egyptian desert. Members of the royal family and other important Egyptians used the valley for burials for around 500 years.

Howard Carter

4

"At first I could see nothing," Carter said. "But . . . details from the room within slowly **emerged** from the mist. Strange animals, statues, and gold—everywhere the glint of gold."

Tutankhamen's tomb had remained hidden in the Valley of the Kings for 3,245 years. Now its ancient secrets were about to be revealed!

This photo shows what Carter likely saw when he first looked into Tut's tomb.

Tutankhamen

Pharaoh Tutankhamen was a part of a powerful **civilization** based in Africa from around 3,000 B.C. to A.D. 300. Experts know he was born around 1341 B.C. They also know Tutankhamen, or Tut for short, was the son of the ancient Egyptian king Akhenaton (*ah*-ken-AHT-on). Tut grew up in a city named after his father.

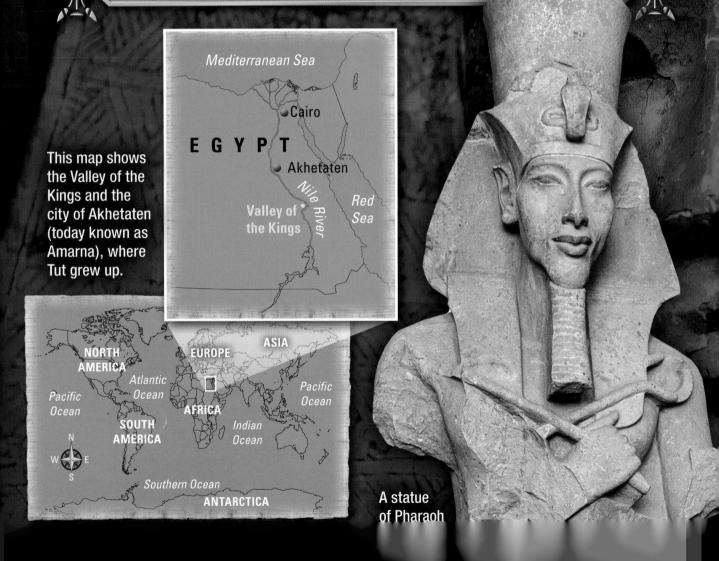

This map shows the Valley of the Kings and the city of Akhetaten (today known as Amarna), where Tut grew up.

A statue of Pharaoh

However, little else is known about the young prince's life. Tut most likely lived in a palace with his father, his father's many wives, and his six older sisters. When Tutankhamen was still a young child, his father died. Then, when Tut was just nine years old, he became pharaoh. As a result, Tutankhamen became known as the boy king.

Queen Nefertiti

Tut married one of his older sisters, named Ankhesenamun. This is an image of the young king and queen.

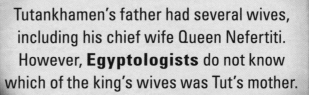

Tutankhamen's father had several wives, including his chief wife Queen Nefertiti. However, **Egyptologists** do not know which of the king's wives was Tut's mother.

The King Is Dead!

Only about ten years after becoming pharaoh, Tutankhamen mysteriously died. After his death, his body was taken to an **embalmers**' workshop. There it would be made into a mummy. In ancient Egypt, people believed in the **afterlife**, or life after death. So they **preserved** a person's body so that he or she could live on in the afterlife.

First, the embalmers drained all the blood from Tut's **corpse**. Then, using their hands, they carefully removed his lungs, liver, stomach, and intestines from a small cut in his **abdomen**.

This embalmer is wearing an Anubis mask. Anubis is the Egyptian god of death and embalmers. He's usually shown with the head of a wild dog.

The ancient Egyptians did not believe the brain was important. To remove it, an embalmer pushed a metal hook up the corpse's nose. Then he pulled the brain out in little pieces.

These organs were placed in salt to dry and preserve them. Then each organ was wrapped in linen and placed in a tiny **coffin**-shaped container. Salt was then heaped over the whole body to dry it. After about 35 days, the embalmers wrapped the dry, shriveled body with strips of cloth to create a mummy.

Before wrapping a body, its dry skin was rubbed with beeswax, animal fat, and plant oils to make it soft again.

A person's heart was often left inside the body. The ancient Egyptians believed that once a person's **spirit** entered the world of the dead, his or her heart was weighed. If a person had a light heart, he or she could enter the afterlife. A heavy heart meant that a person was bad and would be eaten by a monster called the Devourer.

The Devourer was part crocodile, part lion, and part hippo.

To give a dried-out body a plump, lifelike shape, it was packed with linen and sawdust.

The Valley of the Kings

Once Tut's body was mummified, it was placed in a coffin. Then servants carried the preserved corpse into the Valley of the Kings. Here, in a desert cemetery close to his royal **ancestors**, Tutankhamen was placed in an underground tomb. Like all pharaohs, Tut was considered a god who lived on Earth when he was alive. Now, in death, he would take his place alongside other gods in the afterlife.

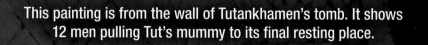

Tut's mummy

This painting is from the wall of Tutankhamen's tomb. It shows 12 men pulling Tut's mummy to its final resting place.

To live on forever, Tut would need food to eat and clothing and jewelry to wear. He might also need furniture, including a throne to sit on and chariots to ride. In addition, Tut may want weapons and entertainment, such as games and musical instruments. Everything a pharaoh could possibly need or want in the afterlife was placed in Tut's tomb. Then the tomb was sealed . . . forever.

An assortment of actual items found in Tut's tomb

A couch with the head of the cow goddess, Mehetweret

These egg-shaped, wooden boxes held meat, including goose and ox tongue.

A shabti statue

Tutankhamen was buried with 412 tiny statues called shabtis. In the afterlife, the shabtis would work for the pharaoh as servants and farmers.

11

Discovery in the Desert

As the centuries passed, the tombs in the Valley of the Kings became hidden under layers of sand and rock. In the 1800s and early 1900s, archaeologists and treasure seekers traveled to Egypt to hunt for ancient tombs and the valuable **artifacts** inside them. However, no one was able to find the lost tomb of the boy king.

Then in early November 1922, archaeologist Howard Carter made a stunning discovery. Beneath the sand and rock, Carter uncovered a flight of 16 steps leading to an underground door.

Entrance to Ramesses VI's tomb

Entrance to Tut's tomb

Tut's tomb was discovered beneath the tomb of Pharaoh Ramesses VI, which was uncovered in 1888.

Carter told his friend and employer, Lord Carnarvon, about the exciting discovery. When Lord Carnarvon arrived in Egypt a few weeks later, Carter continued the **excavation**. Carter soon learned that the underground door led to a passageway filled with rubble. Once the rubble was cleared away, Carter and Lord Carnarvon found themselves standing before the doorway to Tut's tomb.

Lord Carnarvon was a wealthy Englishman who loved ancient Egypt. He hired Howard Carter to search for buried Egyptian tombs.

From left to right: Lady Evelyn Herbert (Carnarvon's daughter), Lord Carnarvon, Howard Carter, and Arthur Callender (Carter's friend and member of the team) on the steps leading to the tomb

Wonderful Things

When Carter looked into Tut's tomb for the first time, Lord Carnarvon asked if he could see anything. "Yes, yes," replied Carter. "It is wonderful!" He was right. Gold statues shined in the candlelight. No one had ever discovered a tomb filled with as many objects as Tutankhamen's.

In the days that followed, Carter and Lord Carnarvon explored different chambers inside the tomb, including the antechamber and the annex. Even though it was tiny, the annex was packed with hundreds of items. Some of the objects included jars of wine and oil, baskets of fruit, and furniture.

A carved stone jar containing oil that came from Tut's tomb

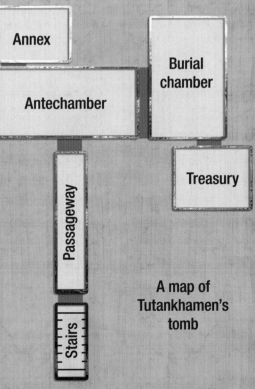

A map of Tutankhamen's tomb

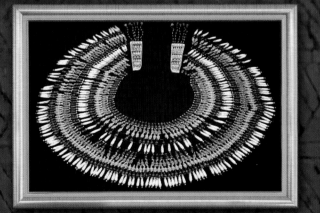

A beaded collar found in Tut's tomb

As he carefully searched the rooms, Carter realized that others had been there before him—tomb robbers! Carter noticed that the tomb's two outer doorways had been broken and repaired. Also, the tiny annex chamber was very messy and looked as though someone had hurriedly searched through it.

In ancient Egypt, thieves would break into tombs to steal the goods inside. Even though guards patrolled the Valley of the Kings, most of the pharaohs' tombs were eventually robbed of their treasures.

Below is a heap of objects found in the annex, which Carter carefully examined and numbered.

Another Sealed Door

Carter knew that the discovery of Tut's tomb could tell the world a lot about life in ancient Egypt. He made sure that every item was photographed and carefully cleaned and checked before it was removed from the tomb. He also made detailed drawings and notes about the artifacts.

Carter found many jewelry boxes in Tut's tomb. The boxes contained lists of their contents. When he checked what he found against the lists, he discovered many items were missing. Carter still found more than 200 pieces of jewelry, though.

A piece of jewelry found in Tut's tomb that's decorated with a blue scarab beetle

This piece of Tut's jewelry shows the Egyptian god Horus, shown as a falcon

Carter soon realized that there was no sign of a mummy in the antechamber or annex. There was, however, another sealed door leading from the antechamber. Next to that door stood two life-size statues of pharaohs covered in gold. Was it possible that there was yet another room? Could Tut's mummy lay just a few feet away?

Carter and Lord Carnarvon carefully removing the sealed door in the antechamber

One of the gold pharaoh statues

Meeting Tutankhamen

When Carter finally opened the sealed door, he couldn't believe his eyes. Behind it he discovered Tut's burial chamber! In the middle of the room stood a huge, **gilded** wooden box, or **shrine**.

When Carter opened the doors at one end of the shrine, he found three smaller shrines inside it. Inside the inner shrine was a stone coffin, or **sarcophagus**. Slowly and carefully over many months, Carter and his workers removed the shrines from the tomb. Then the heavy stone lid of the sarcophagus was raised using ropes and pulleys.

Carter opens the doors of the shrines in the burial chamber.

Inside the sarcophagus were three beautiful coffins, one neatly placed inside the other. Each coffin was made in the shape of the king's body. The third and inner coffin was made of solid gold. When the lid of the golden coffin was opened, Carter found Tut's mummy inside! The mummy's head and shoulders were covered by a dazzling gold mask. Carter was speechless—the boy king had finally been found!

Carter and a worker examine the inner coffin.

Solid gold, inner coffin

Second, or middle, coffin

Tut's gold mask

In ancient Egypt, both men and women wore dark eyeliner. The eyeliner on Tutankhamen's mummy mask is made from a blue rock called lapis lazuli.

The Mummy Autopsy

On November 11, 1925, Carter and a small team of scientists gathered around Tut's mummy to perform an **autopsy**. One of the men, Professor Douglas Derry, led the work. Derry began by making a long cut down the middle of Tut. This allowed the delicate wrappings to be peeled back to reveal the pharaoh's preserved body.

Between the wrappings and on the king's body, the team discovered 150 valuable objects. These included charms called amulets, jeweled collars, bracelets, and two daggers.

These daggers and their covers were found placed against Tutankhamen's thighs.

The gold mummy mask was lifted away with extreme care. Then the wrappings around Tutankhamen's head were removed. The scientists gently examined Tut's dark brown, brittle skin. Carter was finally able to look into the face of the young pharaoh. Derry then examined the mummy's bones and teeth. He confirmed that Tut had died when he was around 19 years old. However, Derry could find no clues as to why the pharaoh had died so young.

Tutankhamen's mummy

A mummy's fingernails and toenails fell off as the skin shriveled. These gold coverings, called stalls, were used to cover Tutankhamen's fingers and toes.

21

Tut's Treasures

Just beyond Tut's burial chamber, Carter and his team found a room called the treasury. In it, they discovered a large **canopic chest**. It was made from a single block of rock. When the chest's lid was removed, it revealed four stoppers. Each was carved in the shape of Tut's head. Beneath each stopper was a hollow space containing a tiny coffin. Inside the coffins were the king's mummified lungs, liver, stomach, and intestines.

canopic chest

Stopper

A small coffin containing one of Tut's mummified organs

More than 5,000 other objects were found throughout Tut's tomb, including model boats, canes, and golden sandals. Carter also found gloves Tut had worn as a child. He even found a lock of hair belonging to Queen Tiye (TEE-ay), Tut's grandmother!

It took Carter almost ten years to examine all the objects and send them to the Cairo Museum. Once there, the objects helped Egyptologists learn about life—and death—in ancient Egypt. However, Carter and his team could still not figure out what happend to Tut.

A wooden sandal decorated with gold

In the treasury, Carter found two tiny golden coffins. Each coffin held a mummified baby girl. Scientists believe the babies were Tutankhamen's daughters, who died at birth.

A box discovered in the treasury

How Did Tut Die?

For almost 100 years, Egyptologists have wanted to know what killed Tutankhamen. After examining his body and skull, scientists discovered several broken bones. They looked into whether a blow to the head or a chariot crash might have killed Tut.

Then, in 2014, scientists carried out a **virtual autopsy** of Tut. They examined more than 2,000 **CT scans** of Tutankhamen's remains. The scientists discovered that damage to Tut's skull and other **fractures** actually happened after his death. The breaks may have occurred when Howard Carter moved the fragile mummy.

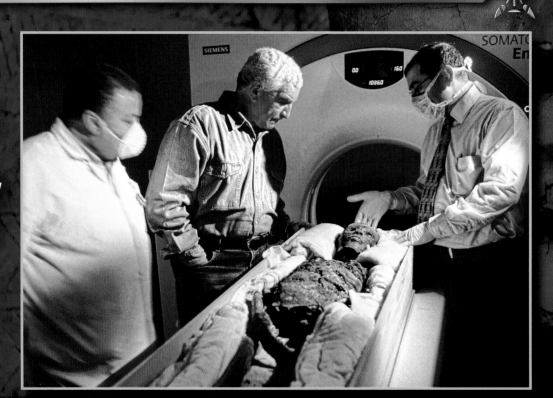

Tut's mummy ready to be scanned in a CT machine

The scans also showed a bad fracture on Tut's left knee that happened shortly before he died. Tests have also shown that Tut had a disease called malaria. No one knows for sure, but perhaps this illness—and a serious infection from his knee injury—killed the young king.

The scientists also discovered that Tut had a badly disfigured left foot. He likely used a cane to get around. Tut probably was unable to stand up and ride in a chariot because of the foot.

This painting from Tut's tomb shows him riding in a chariot. In the afterlife, he would be able to do things he couldn't do when he was alive.

Mysteries of the Tomb

There are signs within Tut's tomb that suggest he died suddenly. Unlike most pharaohs' tombs, Tutankhamen's was very small and had little decoration. Usually, a pharaoh's tomb would take years to build and decorate. When Tut died unexpectedly, was his official tomb not ready? Is it possible his small, simple tomb was prepared at the last minute?

It normally took years for artists to paint an ancient Egyptian king's tomb. However, Tut's tomb paintings were rushed and likely painted in just a few days.

Today, Tut's mummy lies in the antechamber of his tomb

The walls of Tut's tomb are covered with dark spots of ancient mold. This suggests that the room was once damp. This mold does not appear in any other pharaoh's tomb. Was the tomb sealed up before the wall paintings had dried?

In 2012, special photographs were taken of the burial chamber, and the mystery took a new turn. Experts noticed traces of two blocked-up doorways in the walls. In 2015, scientists used high-tech **radar** to scan the walls. They discovered what looks like additional chambers. Are there more rooms beyond Tutankhamen's burial chamber? Is it possible that his small tomb was built in the entrance to a much larger tomb? And, if so, who does it belong to? The investigation continues. . . .

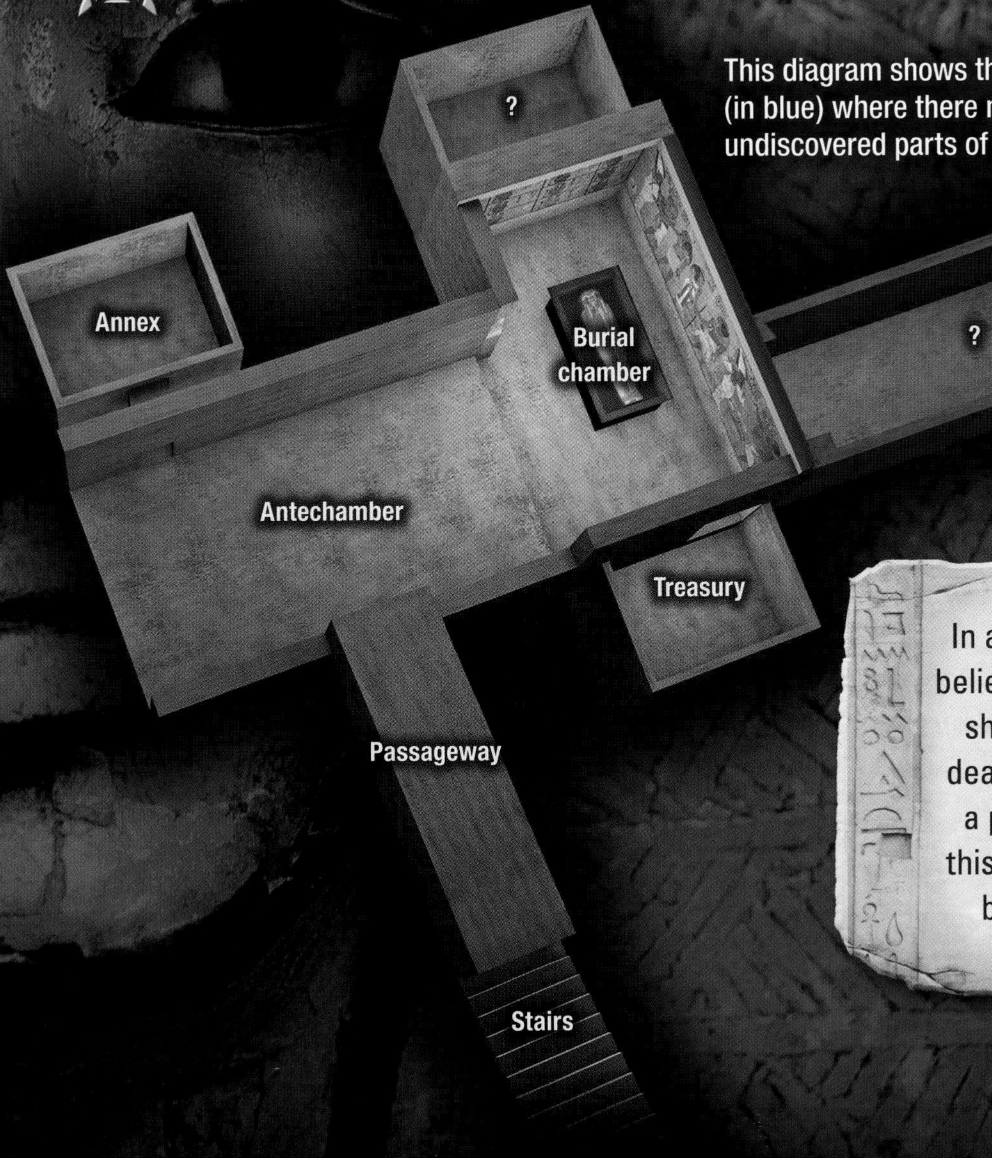

This diagram shows the areas (in blue) where there may be undiscovered parts of the tomb.

?

Annex

Burial chamber

?

Antechamber

Treasury

Passageway

In ancient Egypt, it was believed that only 70 days should pass between death and the sealing of a person's tomb. Was this why Tutankhamen's burial was rushed?

Stairs

Egypt's Ancient Secrets

Howard Carter's discovery of Tutankhamen's tomb revealed many ancient secrets. It also unearthed some exciting mysteries that remain until this day.

Who Was the Owner of the Golden Mask?

In recent times, scientists have studied Tutankhamen's gold mask and discovered that the gold on the face is a different kind of gold than the gold on the rest of the mask. Was the mask originally made for someone else? Was Tut's face added later?

Tut or Nefertiti?

In Tutankhamen's time, the heads on the stoppers of the containers in a canopic chest were carved to look like the owner. Yet the faces on Tut's stoppers do not look like the young king. In fact, they look more like a woman. Some experts think they look like Queen Nefertiti. Yet why would Tut's organs be in containers made for Nefertiti?

Canopic stopper

Where is Queen Nefertiti?

Experts know from various artifacts that Queen Nefertiti was a powerful figure in ancient Egypt. However, her tomb and mummy have never been found. Is Nefertiti's tomb still waiting to be discovered? Is it possible that her tomb lies beyond Tut's burial chamber? Was the entrance to Nefertiti's tomb used as a burial place for Tut after he died suddenly? Were items taken from her tomb and then reused for the young pharaoh?

Queen Nefertiti

Who is the Mummy's Mummy?

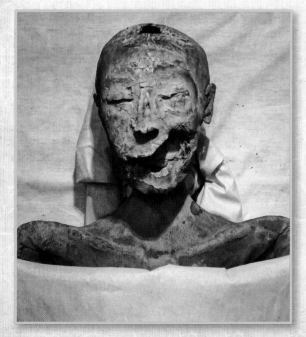

In 1898, the mummy of a young woman was discovered in a tomb in the Valley of the Kings. She was found next to a mummy of a much older woman. The older mummy turned out to be Tutankhamen's grandmother Queen Tiye. Later, scientists used **DNA tests** to prove that the young woman was Tut's mother. No one knows her name, however.

Tut's mother is known as the "Younger Lady" mummy.

Glossary

abdomen (AB-duh-muhn) the part of the body between the neck and hips

afterlife (AF-tur-*life*) the life a person has after he or she dies

ancestors (AN-cess-turz) family members who lived a long time ago

archaeologist (*ar*-kee-OL-uh-jist) a scientist who learns about ancient times by studying things he or she digs up

artifacts (ART-uh-*fakts*) historic objects that were made by people

autopsy (AW-top-see) a detailed examination of a dead body

canopic chest (kuh-NOP-ik CHEST) a decorative box that contains the mummified organs of a dead person

civilization (siv-uh-luh-ZAY-shun) a highly developed society

coffin (KAWF-in) a long box used to hold a dead person

corpse (KORPS) a dead body

CT scans (SEE TEE SCANS) highly detailed X-ray images taken of a body; CT stands for computerized tomography

DNA tests (DEE EN AY TESTS) tests to identify a person by studying his or her DNA (Deoxyribonucleic acid); DNA is unique to each person, except for identical twins

Egyptologists (ee-jip-TOL-uh-jists) historians who specialize in studying ancient Egypt

embalmers (em-BALHM-urz) people who prepare dead bodies for burial

emerged (ih-MURJD) appeared

excavation (eks-*kuh*-VAY-shuhn) the uncovering or digging up of an archaeological site

fractures (FRAK-churz) breaks or cracks in bones

gilded (GILD-id) covered with gold

pharaoh (FAIR-oh) a ruler of ancient Egypt

preserved (pri-ZURVD) treated something to stop it from rotting

radar (RAY-dar) a system that finds objects using radio waves

sarcophagus (sar-KOF-uh-guhss) a stone box made for holding a coffin

shrine (SHRINE) a room, building, or container that holds something special

spirit (SPIHR-it) the part of a person that may live on after death

tense (TENSS) nervous

tomb (TOOM) a grave, room, or building in which a dead body is buried

virtual autopsy (VUR-choo-uhl AW-top-see) an autopsy carried out on a computer by examining X-rays of a dead body

Bibliography

Hawass, Zahi. *Tutankhamen: The Mystery of the Boy King.* Washington, DC: National Geographic (2005).

Reeves, Nicholas. *The Complete Tutankhamen: The King, the Tomb, the Royal Treasure.* London: Thames and Hudson (1990).

Reeves, Nicholas, and Richard H. Wilkinson. *The Complete Valley of the Kings: Tombs and Treasures of Egypt's Greatest Pharaohs.* London: Thames and Hudson (1996).

Read More

Carlson Asselin, Kristine. *Pharaohs and Dynasties of Ancient Egypt (Fact Finders).* North Mankato, MN: Capstone (2012).

Lunis, Natalie. *Tut's Deadly Tomb (HorrorScapes).* New York: Bearport (2011).

Owen, Ruth. *How to Make an Egyptian Mummy (It's a Fact!).* New York: Ruby Tuesday Books (2015).

Learn More Online

To learn more about King Tut and his tomb, visit
www.bearportpublishing.com/EgyptsAncientSecrets

Index

About the Author

Ruth Owen has written many nonfiction books for children.
She has always been fascinated by ancient Egyptian history
and the work of archaeologists.